If You Lived During the Plimoth Thanksgiving

Written By
Chris Newell
Illustrated By
Winona Nelson

With special thanks to Linda Coombs (Aquinnah Wampanoag).

Library of Congress Cataloging-in-Publication Data available

ISBN 978-1-338-72636-7 (paperback) / ISBN 978-1-338-72637-4 (hardcover)

10 9 8 7 6 5 4 3 23 24 25 26 27

Printed in China 38
First edition, October 2021

Book design by Jaime Lucero and Brian LaRossa

If You Lived
During the Plimoth Thanksgiving

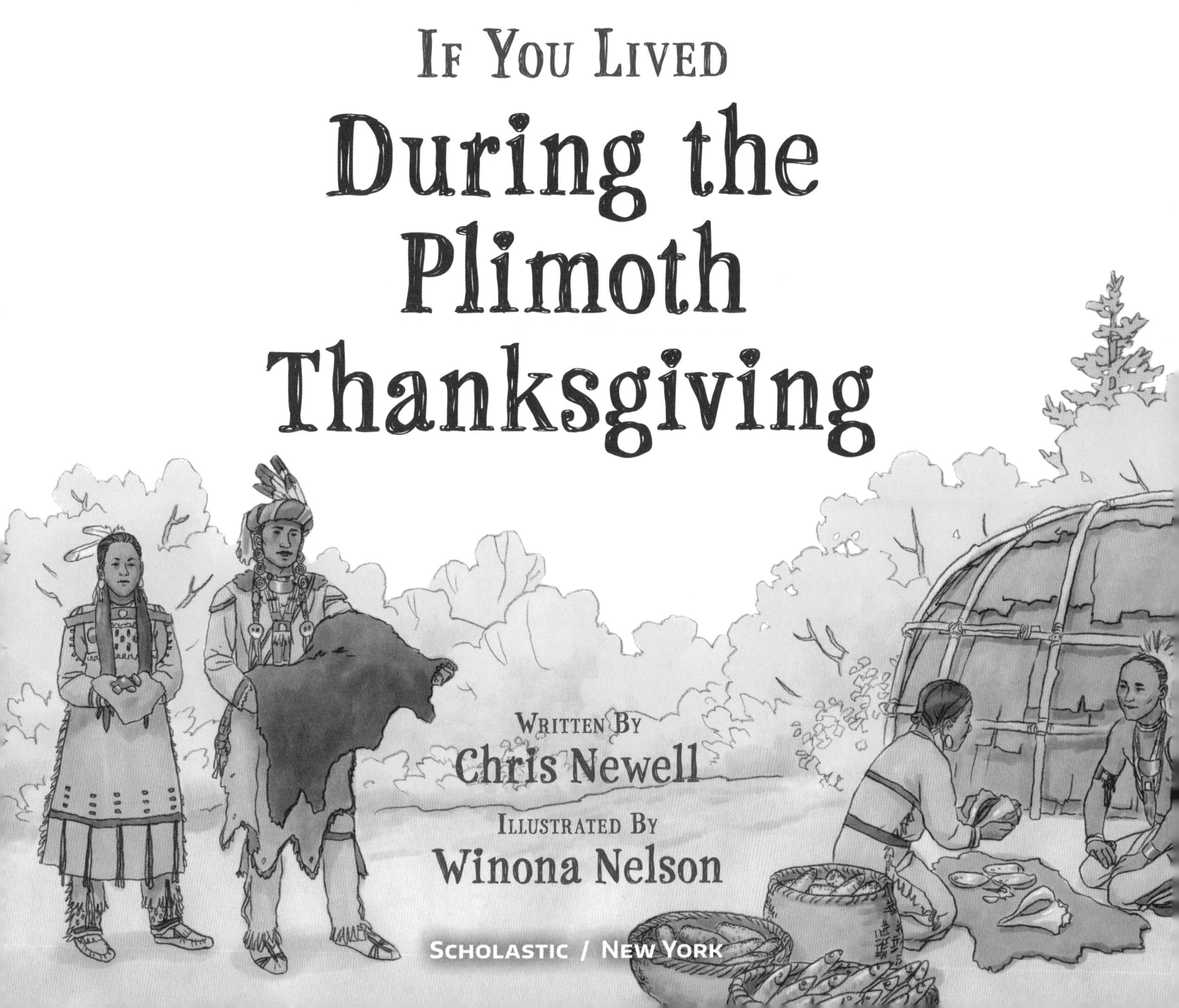

Written By
Chris Newell
Illustrated By
Winona Nelson

Scholastic / New York

Table of Contents

Introduction

The "First Thanksgiving" has become a **foundational** story of how America came to be. The *Mayflower* landing in Plimoth in 1620 and the later feast in 1621 are taught as a turning point in the creation of a new country. However, the holiday we celebrate today does not have any real connection to the *Mayflower's* landing. In fact, the story that links them was not created until two hundred years later. Nevertheless, it is important to understand the events of this critical landing.

The creation of the English settlement at Patuxet (Plimoth) established a foothold in the region for English **colonization**. The country we know as the United States is based largely on the culture and history of **colonists** who arrived from England. They came to settle and control territory and to harvest the vast resources of the American continent to gain wealth. Later, thirteen English colonies on the eastern coast banded together as "Americans," leading to historical events such as the American Revolution and the establishment of the US Constitution.

Those events are only part of the story. Before the arrival of any Europeans, Native peoples lived in America by the millions. Entire nations of people connected by land, kinship, language, and culture existed on the continent for more than twelve thousand years. The story of the *Mayflower* as a foundational myth of the country's beginning erases the harsh realities of disease and aggression experienced by Native peoples as Europeans settled their colonies in America. It also erases the current existence of Native peoples who live in the United States today. The *Mayflower* landing is an important piece of history that needs exploration. But in its exploration, all perspectives should be sought. The story of the *Mayflower* landing is different depending on whether the storyteller viewed the events from the boat or from the shore.

What was the *Mayflower* voyage?

The *Mayflower* voyage was the journey of English colonists on a ship called the *Mayflower* in 1620. The passengers intended to establish a new plantation within the English-occupied **colony** of Virginia, 500 miles south of Plimoth. The Virginia Colony was controlled by the Virginia Company and was settled in 1607. This voyage was originally made up of two ships: Captain Christopher Jones's *Mayflower of London* was the cargo ship that

set off alongside a boat called the *Speedwell*. Both were bound to cross the Atlantic Ocean in 1620.

Shortly after they began their journey, the *Speedwell* sprang a leak that required repair. Both ships returned to England, but the repairs were slow and took nearly a month. After they departed again, another leak opened on the *Speedwell*. It was late in the year, and with no time to wait for repairs, passengers and supplies on the *Speedwell* were transferred to the *Mayflower*. The *Mayflower* set sail again by itself in September, carrying 102 passengers and forty-eight to fifty crew members, as well as supplies and cargo. The voyage lasted sixty-six days.

DID YOU KNOW?

Under the reign of King James I in England, there were twenty-six ships named the *Mayflower* in English port books. To distinguish them from one another, they were often referred to by their captain or owner and their home port.

When and where did the *Mayflower* land?

The *Mayflower* finally left Plymouth, England, on September 16, 1620. The monthlong delay put the ship at the mercy of dangerous winds and storms common at that time of year. William Bradford, governor of the Plimoth Colony in 1621, wrote that the storms were so bad that one of the crew was swept off the ship by a giant wave. As a result of the stormy conditions, the ship became lost near the end of the journey. It landed far north of the Virginia Colony, its intended destination. Instead, the ship arrived in Wampanoag territory at the village of Meeshawm, in what is now known as Provincetown, Massachusetts. Nearly out of supplies and in dire need of food and fresh water, the passengers explored the area for resources. They had their first sighting of

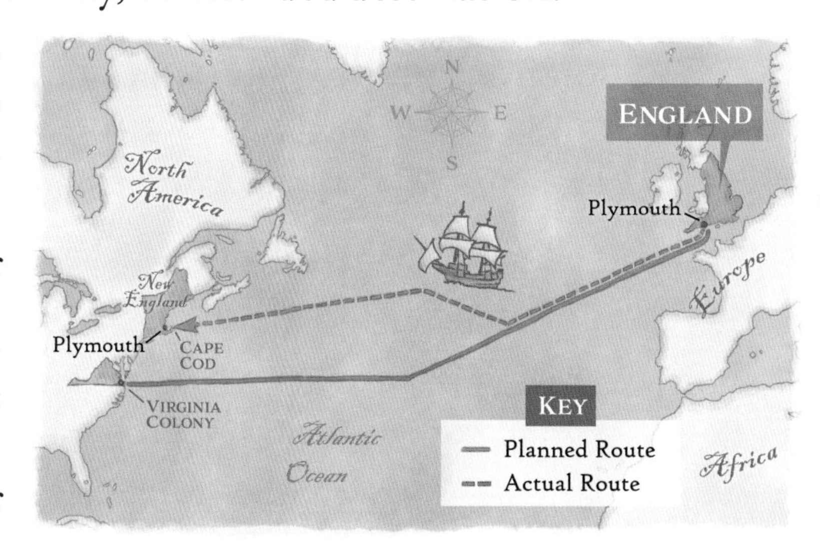

several Meeshawm people a ways down the beach.

The English continued exploring and went down to the territory of the Nauset Wampanoag, where six years before another ship had kidnapped twenty people to be sold into the Native slave trade. Upon seeing the arrival of the English pulling ashore, several Nauset men ran out and began shooting arrows at them, thinking they were one more ship coming to steal hostages.

They quickly forced them back to their ship, and the colonists began another search for a suitable landing area.

Nearly starved and out of supplies, they navigated the ship across the bay until they found a safe harbor in the area of the Wampanoag village of Patuxet. When the English landed in Patuxet, they found the remains of a recently abandoned village.

The previous villagers had perished from an illness brought by Europeans years before. The sickness wiped out more than three-quarters of the coastal population. It spread from the shores of what is now Maine, traveled down the coast to the Patuxet area, turned inland, and stopped at Narragansett Bay. These years are known to some tribes in the region as the Great Dying of 1616–1619.

With winter fast approaching, the passengers of Captain Jones's *Mayflower* chose to settle in Patuxet. They would rename their settlement Plimoth Plantation (present-day Plymouth, Massachusetts). The names Plimoth and Plymouth are pronounced the same and refer to the same place in America, even though they are spelled differently.

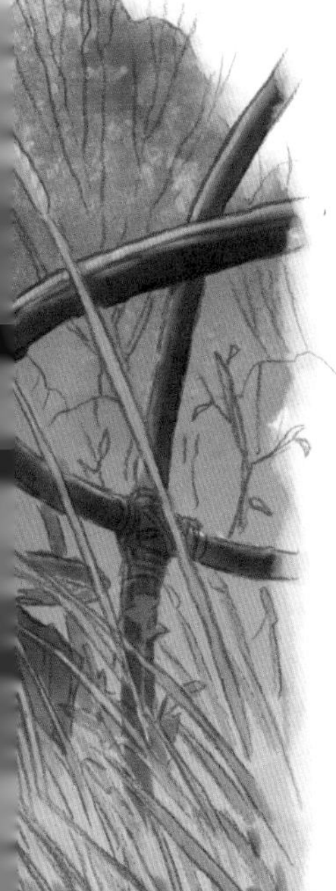

DID YOU KNOW?

The English commonly used the labels "Indians" or "savages" to describe the multiple nations of peoples and cultures they encountered in America. "Savages" was incredibly demeaning. Even though the terms were inaccurate and dehumanizing, they became familiar in English terminology. Today the language has changed and generalized terms like "American Indian," "Native American," "First Nation," "Indigenous," or "Native" are all in use. However, Native peoples prefer to be called by their tribe or nation whenever possible.

What is a colony, and who is a colonist?

A colony is land occupied in a foreign territory. The "foreign territories" are the homelands of other peoples whose lives and cultures are completely disrupted as their lands are taken over. When a country wants to move its people into a foreign land, they begin by establishing a land base, or settlement, for their people. Colonists are the people who leave their homeland to settle in the new colony. For this reason, colonists are also sometimes called settlers.

In 1493, Pope Alexander VI issued a decree called *Inter Caetara*, often called the "Doctrine of Discovery." In it, he declared that European explorers like Christopher Columbus had the right to claim any lands they "**discovered**" in their

monarch's name. Any European explorer could land on and claim territory not already controlled by a Christian monarch. They planted a flag, reported back to the king or queen who sponsored the journey about their newly discovered land, and then occupied it. This is how people began to "own" land in America. European explorers used the Doctrine of Discovery to justify control of the land they "discovered," as well as its vast and rich resources.

In the 1600s, Europeans were already creating settlements on the eastern coast of the American continent. The French started colonies in what is now Canada, and the Dutch established colonies in what is now Connecticut and New York. The English established colonies in Virginia and Massachusetts and later along the entire east coast of America. The intent was to take control of territory by any means in order to profit from selling the

DID YOU KNOW?

The Doctrine of Discovery of 1493 is still used in American law to justify the United States government's ownership and control of Native homelands.

plentiful resources back to Europe.

Early European ships came for the high-quality North Atlantic cod. Codfish were a rich source of food and wealth for European fishermen. As they settled on the land, colonists began selling other American resources to Europe. They harvested and sold large, old-growth trees for building material; beaver fur to make hats; tobacco; and anything else they considered valuable or profitable.

DID YOU KNOW?

To discover something is to find it first and then make it known to others. Indigenous peoples occupied the American continent for more than twelve thousand years before Europeans arrived. Europeans did not begin occupying it until the 1500s—less than six hundred years ago. Using "discover" to describe European arrival and settlement in the Americas is not accurate. Still, the English colonists used the term to give themselves ownership of American lands under their own law.

Who were the Pilgrims?

A **pilgrim** is a person who makes a long journey to a foreign land, often for religious purposes. In 1608, a group of English citizens, unhappy with the Church of England, protested by leaving for Holland (present-day Netherlands) to practice Christianity freely as they chose. These people were known as religious separatists because of their wish to separate themselves from the large, established, organized churches of the time. However, life for the separatists was difficult in Holland. Many of the separatists also disagreed on how their religion should be practiced. As a result, a group of like-minded separatists made plans to leave Holland for the American continent.

In 1620, forty-one members of this group returned to England on a ship called the *Speedwell.* They had dreams of going to America. The separatists referred to themselves as "Saints." William Bradford, the future leader of their new settlement at Plimoth Plantation, was one of the Saints. In his journal, which was later published in a two-part book called *Of Plimoth Plantation*, he called their journey a pilgrimage. When describing leaving England, he wrote, "They knew they were pilgrims, and looked not much on those things, but lift[ed] up their eyes to the heavens, their dearest country; and quieted their spirits." The term "pilgrim" referred to the forty-one self-named Saints until the 1800s, when it became common in America to refer to all passengers on Captain Jones's *Mayflower* as Pilgrims, whether they were Saints or not.

Who else was on the *Mayflower*?

Saints joined a much larger group of mostly nonreligious fortune seekers, including sixty-two passengers and forty-eight to fifty crew members. The Saints referred to this group as "Strangers."

All passengers were familiar with the Christian religion, having been raised as part of the Church of England. Some of them were faithful to their church and some were not. Some were indentured servants paying a debt to another passenger. For Strangers, religion and the freedom to worship as they saw fit were not the main reasons they were going to America, although they welcomed the freedom.

When the *Mayflower* made its first landing near Cape Cod, Massachusetts, tensions were high between the Saints and Strangers, and they began to argue and take sides against one another. The Pilgrims understood that they needed to create a government for the good of all on the ship. In November 1620, they signed a document titled "An Agreement Between the Settlers at New Plymouth" that we now know as the

***Mayflower* Compact**. This established a temporary set of laws for the new settlement, and was signed by forty-one adult male English colonists, including two indentured servants.

The agreements were:

- The colonists would live by their Christian faith.
- They would make laws for the good of the colony and abide by them.
- They would create one society and work together to further it.
- Despite self-governing, they were loyal subjects to King James I.

It was not until a month later, in December, that the *Mayflower* finally landed in Plimoth Bay, where the colonists began building their new settlement. Regardless of whether they

were Saints or Strangers, all the people aboard Captain Jones's *Mayflower* had a tough first winter in their new plantation. As they built their new homes, they were living on the ship and wading ashore. Without the proper supplies, nearly half of them died.

Why did English colonists come to America?

Every European colonist came to America for different reasons. Many were motivated by the idea of creating new lives. Forming colonies also expanded the wealth of European countries, as well as their influence on the world. Like other European countries, the English wished to gain control of all Indigenous lands in the Americas, including any resources that the land held, such as timber or furs.

In England, people owned plots of land and worked those plots to make their resources. Having land did not only mean raising crops for food. It also meant making "improvements," the English term for changing the land to suit their needs. These improvements created extra resources, which they sold using the concept of **currency**. At the time, currency came in the form of coins—equally weighted valuable metals. People exchanged their surplus goods for coins or traded for goods like tobacco. Under this system, people measured wealth by the amount of currency they obtained and kept, as many cultures still do today.

The Native cultures the English encountered in America did not practice the same system of land ownership by individual people. Instead, many saw their homelands as animate life. The land and waters of Native homelands are seen as a system that can be maintained to provide resources for all. Instead of individuals owning, caring for, and "improving" a plot of land, Native communities shared areas of land that naturally created all the needed resources for food, clothing, and shelter.

These cultures adapted to the most successful life systems for the land they occupied, whether it was fishing, hunting, gathering, farming, or trade. In these systems, maintaining the natural balance of the land, rather than making changes or "improvements," had a much higher value. An individual's wealth was not measured by how much currency they accumulated, but by how much they contributed to the life-giving systems that sustained their communities.

Who were the people the English colonists encountered in Patuxet?

Patuxet is the Wampanoag village area that the Pilgrims finally chose to settle in, renaming it Plimoth. The Great Dying of 1616–1619 hit the people at Patuxet especially hard, and all of them perished. When the *Mayflower* arrived at Patuxet, the English found only what remained of a once thriving village. There were cleared lands for planting, now overgrown; many houses now falling apart; and the remains of those who died in the plague.

As the English colonists began exploring the area in late December of 1620, they heard people in the distance. These were Wampanoag people, the People of the First Light. They had been watching the Pilgrims' entire journey through Meeshawm and Nauset on Cape Cod. The Wampanoag stayed safely far away, but the English on many occasions could hear the noise of several people in the woods, making their presence known.

The Wampanoag people are a confederacy of coastal tribes who share common cultural and language bonds. They are known as People of the First Light because their homelands are on the east coast of North America, so they are among the first tribes to see the sunrise every morning. The Wampanoag people and their ancestors had lived around Patuxet, in what is now eastern Massachusetts, in the part of Rhode Island on the eastern side of Narragansett Bay, and also on Cape Cod and the nearby islands.

The Wampanoag nation at one time included sixty-nine villages. Each village had their own leader, and within the territory of each there were winter village sites where everyone lived together in longhouses. In the summer, each family spread out to their respective planting sites, where they grew corn, beans, and squash. There was much overlap between

these villages, and often people from different villages or tribal groups intermarried.

After marriage, the local custom was for the husband to move to his wife's village and become part of her community. Native peoples in the region traced their lineage through their mother—the opposite of the English custom of taking a father's last name and tracing lineage through him. If a husband and wife had children, the children would be known as members of the mother's community, regardless of where their father was born. In this societal structure, women helped govern their communities. The leaders of the villages were called sachems (SAY-chem). While they were often men, there were many female sachems as well. Leaders were chosen from the sachem family by the clan mothers of the village, if not by direct descent.

Wampanoag leaders knew from experience that the large wooden ships from Europe sometimes meant big trouble. The English settlers on the *Mayflower* did not announce their arrival to the Wampanoag people. There was no contact or communication with any Wampanoag leadership to arrange for their arrival and settlement. It is usual for people from one country to negotiate with the leaders of another country before settling there. The English did not believe that they needed to do this when coming to Wampanoag country.

Wampanoag people kept a close watch on what the English were doing, but they did not approach. While in Meeshawm, the colonists had dug up a mound of earth while searching for food and water. It turned out to be a grave, and they took many of the items that were buried with the person before covering it back up. The English next discovered a family's food storage pit and proceeded to take six bushels of corn for their own use. In the site now called Plimoth, the English were harvesting wood and sawing boards to begin constructing their homes. The Wampanoag saw all of this and waited through the winter before deciding whether it was safe to approach. The Wampanoag people and the English settlers would not meet for another three months.

How did early encounters with other European ships affect Native peoples in the area?

European ships had been showing up in Wampanoag territory for nearly one hundred years before the arrival of the *Mayflower*. Portuguese, Spanish, French, and English fishermen were already fishing for highly valued and prized North Atlantic cod off the northeast coast of North America. These ships were coming into the area, filling their hulls with fish and whales, and then taking them back to their home countries in Europe to sell. Sometimes, encounters with these ships were friendly; sometimes they were not. It depended on the ship and its captain's intentions.

Along with fishing ships came slave ships. The abominable practice of slavery was common in certain parts of the world during the 1500s and 1600s. The average price for the sale of an enslaved Native person was about 220 shillings in England, which was a large amount of money. Because of this, many Native peoples were extremely suspicious of any ships they saw coming to their shores.

The earliest written records of these encounters came from explorers in the 1500s searching the coast for resources and for ocean passages that might let them travel to Asia. Italian navigator Giovanni da Verrazzano was one of those explorers, traveling the coast for King Francis I of France and writing his observances as early as 1524. When he arrived in Narragansett territory, he wrote very kindly of the Native peoples he encountered. "This is the finest looking tribe, and the handsomest," he wrote. He described the men's

bodies as larger in size than the men on his ship, and all in good proportion. He wrote, "Their women are of the same form and beauty, very graceful."

Verrazzano continued to write about the friendly nature of the Native peoples in the region. He made note of their use of copper, which was refined and worn as ornaments on hair, as necklaces, or on clothing. They valued the reddish-brown copper over the yellow-colored gold on his ship. While trading for Native goods, he found that gold was the least desired metal of his trade goods. Verrazzano went ashore and saw a well-maintained landscape of forest and open areas "adapted to cultivation of every kind." He wrote that the woods were full of large trees that were unknown to him. He saw new fruits of all kinds, and he wrote about how the people hunted or snared "[t]he animals, which are in great numbers."

Verrazzano traveled farther up the coast to what is now the state of Maine. Native peoples there had already seen European ships, and were not so friendly to his arrival. Verrazzano tried in vain to make a close connection with the Wabanaki tribes of the area. They were wary of his ship and would only trade by using a long cord lowered from high rocks to the boat, so that no one had physical contact with one another. While Verrazzano described friendly encounters, some tribes had already learned about the negative outcomes of encountering a wooden ship such as his. By 1620, all the Native peoples in the region were cautious of these newcomers.

Ships that came only to trade or fish also brought diseases from Europe that were entirely new to Native peoples. Epidemics spread up and down the coast, affecting the Wampanoag and other coastal tribes. Patuxet, where the *Mayflower* landed, had fallen victim to the Great Dying a few years before. Few, if any, survived. If there were survivors, they would have fled to another village. As a result of a devastation like this, Native peoples understood the deadly risk of new diseases from Europe.

What other people lived in this area?

The entire eastern coastal region, as well as the interior of the continent, was well populated by different Native peoples in 1620. The boundaries between the different nations, and the villages or communities within them, were marked by natural features such as rivers, ponds, hills, or mountains. People respected one another's territories and followed certain protocols when going into other people's homelands.

The homelands of a group of people defined the language, culture, and way of life. Besides the Wampanoag people, there were several other tribal nations in the region near Patuxet.

Above the North River on the coast were the Massachusett, who associated with the "great foothill" areas of their homeland. To the west were the Nipmuc peoples, whose name describes their freshwater lake culture in what is now Massachusetts, Rhode Island, and northeastern Connecticut. Along the coast to the south were the Narragansett tribes. Their name comes from the word *nahaganset*, which describes "the people of the small point," from their homeland next to a large and bountiful **estuary**.

What language do Wampanoag people speak, and how did they record history?

The Wampanoag language is called Wôpanâôt8âôk. It is one of a large group of languages that make up the Algonquin language family. Eastern Algonquin-speaking tribes do not all have the same language, but they were similar enough in 1620 to allow people from different tribes to communicate with each other. People naturally spoke more than one language in the Algonquin family, as they were always in contact with one another through travel, trade, marriage, and family, among other reasons.

The vast range of Algonquin-speaking peoples allowed tribes to communicate and trade over great distances using well-known trails and waterways. The Wampanoag language was always an oral language, and was not written down until recently. Everything is described and understood very differently than in English.

Wampanoag peoples did not write their history down on

paper as the English did. Instead, the earliest record is found in the memorization of songs and stories that described their peoples' creation and history. These stories taught them lessons on how they were supposed to treat one another and the land. They described journeys over distances of hundreds of miles in precise detail. For twelve thousand years, these stories formed and changed, preserving the people's living memory and their relationship to their homeland. The songs and stories passed from one generation to the next. This art form survived for thousands of years.

The Wampanoag people also used petroglyphs to record history. Petroglyphs are pictures carved or "pecked" into rocks that help preserve memories or stories. Human-made groupings of stones marked trails and sacred areas. The placement helped track the moon and stars throughout the year. From careful observation, Wampanoag and other Native peoples understood the annual cycle of a year. They based their calendar year on the thirteen lunar cycles, or the thirteen times the moon made the twenty-eight-day orbit around the planet. The system was exact, and as a result, the scientists of Wampanoag culture knew exactly when resources from nature were available. They were also master farmers and predicted the best times to plant their crops to get the most food from them.

Tribes throughout the region created long strands and belts from shell beads known as wampum. People had always used shell

beads for jewelry. After contact with Europeans in the 1500s, Native peoples traded with them for metal awls and nails, which they then fashioned into drills. The metal drills could make smaller holes, so they could make smaller beads.

Wampum beads are seashell beads that are purple and white. The purple beads come from the shiny purple outer edge of the quahog clam shell found in present-day Cape Cod and Long Island Sound. The white beads come from the center stem of spiraled white whelk shells. Wampum belts were made with both colors, with various symbols or images woven in to create their meaning. These belts held great importance and had many different uses. They could record tribal history or events, make laws, or offer condolence.

The historians of the tribe had the skills to interpret the imagery of the belts in detail. Wampum belts were documents used to establish and maintain good relations with all the people who made them. Wampum-producing tribes used wampum as a way to underscore the meaning of truth. It had a vital significance to many Native peoples even beyond their homelands.

What language did the colonists speak, and how did they record history?

The colonists who arrived on the *Mayflower* departed from England and spoke the English language. In 1620, only people who lived in or visited England spoke English. This language was foreign to the Americas. The English language is not like the Wampanoag language, and people from England viewed the world very differently. In English, colonists could "own" an individual plot of land and change it how they wished. This concept was new to Native peoples.

The English commonly used paper documents to record their history and important events. They wrote with quill pens that they dipped in ink. Paper documents and handwritten books were standard all over Europe. Not unlike the use of wampum, paper documents recorded histories, laws, and treaties. Unlike wampum, paper documents (like maps and deeds) also determined who owned which lands.

When the English arrived at Plimoth, they recorded their form of self-governance on a paper document. Colonists wrote the history of Plimoth in famous books like William Bradford's *Of Plimoth Plantation* and (with Edward Winslow) *Mourt's Relation*. The books give a valuable view of how the English saw the events of Plimoth in the 1600s.

What did life for Wampanoag people look like when the *Mayflower* arrived?

In the 1600s, Wampanoag people lived a life that followed the natural life cycles of plant and animal life around them. The sixty-nine villages located in the region (now southeastern Massachusetts and eastern Rhode Island) thrived from making sustainable use of the abundant resources available to them.

In the worldview of the Wampanoag, the land is a maternal force that has the power to give life. Care for the land was the responsibility of the women of the village, and Wampanoag

women took this duty very seriously. They produced a large percentage of the village's food. As a result, women held strong decision-making power.

Young men mainly focused on seasonal hunting and fishing duties, as well as on protecting the village when necessary. Fishing methods were complex. Wampanoag fisherman did not use fishing poles but instead used hook and line, dip nets, spears, seine nets, and harpoons. They also built wooden fences in the water, called "weirs," that worked by taking advantage of the natural movement of their desired catch. The weirs directed the fish to shallower waters, where they became trapped in these large, circular enclosures. For

larger fish and for transportation, tribes in the region created boats by burning out large logs and then shaping them with stone tools into long canoes called *mishoons*.

Hunting was also the job of the men. They used longbows, which were carved from the wood of local trees like maple or ash, and had strings made from the sinew, or tendons, of large animals. The arrows had sharp tips that they made from certain types of hard stone that could be flaked or shaped, in a process called **flint knapping**. Deer and black bear were the largest prey animals in the area. Native hunters guaranteed an excellent hunt by building, like the fishing weirs, deer traps in the woods out of long fences and driving deer through these openings to waiting hunters. Dogs were sometimes pets and protectors and helped the hunt.

A family lived in a home called a wetu, which was a dome-shaped structure covered in bark or cattail reeds depending on the season. Each house had a framework tall enough that you could stand up inside. Thin cedar trees, or saplings, were cut in the springtime when the sap was rising in the tree, which made them easy to bend. They might be soaked in the river or pond to keep them that way while the house was being built.

The thick end of the saplings went into the ground to create the outline of the wetu. Then, they were bent inward to overlap each other and tied together at the higher end with strips of bark peeled from the saplings cut for the frame.

Once the frame was firmly bound together, large sheets of waterproof bark were tied down to cover the home against winter weather. There was a hole in the top to vent smoke from a small fire pit inside. Woven with different colors and patterns, bulrush mats heated or cooled the homes, depending on the season or whether there was a fire inside.

During the hotter summer months, large mats of cattail reeds rather than sheets of bark covered the wetu. This kept them waterproof on rainy days, but airy and shady on hot days. No matter the season, every wetu was full of cups, bowls, pots, baskets, fur blankets, toys, and other household goods.

Whether male or female, young or old, all Wampanoag people worked for the good of their village, and the welfare of the village depended on preserving nature's systems. By following the natural cycles of life in everything around them, the Wampanoag and other tribes adapted and thrived for thousands of years before the arrival of European ships.

What foods were Wampanoag and other Native peoples eating in 1620?

Wampanoag people produced food by growing, gathering, hunting, and fishing, depending on the time of year. Food gathering, processing, and production followed a yearly cycle. As the thirteen lunar cycles progressed, familiar signs from nature told the Wampanoag valuable information. They knew when to find certain kinds of fish, when to plant, and when to gather the natural food resources of the land.

In the summer, Wampanoag people moved from forest areas to lake, river, and ocean shores. Some moved to large, shallow bays, where the freshwater rivers emptied into the salty ocean water. The water in these areas was a mixture of fresh and salt water called **brackish water**. These large areas of shallow brackish water formed estuaries. In the spring, the alewives, or river herring, ran up the rivers by the millions to spawn. The sound of chirping frogs alerted people that mud had softened from the cold winter and the hibernating eels had emerged.

Throughout warmer months, Wampanoag people harvested fish, a dependable source of food.

The Wampanoag harvested resources from the ocean with success and wasted very little. Enormous piles of discarded seashells, a kind of "midden," are proof of the thousands of years in which Wampanoag people thrived from abundant ocean resources.

In spring, the growing season began. Wampanoag people, like many other Native peoples, grew a combination of corn, beans, and squash. When planted together, this is a life-sustaining vegetable combination that yields bigger crops. This is now called **complementary farming**, which the tribes mastered over a thousand years. These three crops were known to tribes in the region as "the three sisters."

Corn is a domestic plant invented in the Americas. Originating in present-day Central America and Mexico, Indigenous agricultural scientists began inventing corn about eight thousand years ago. They **hybridized** a grass called teosinte, which grows a small cob with kernels but is not very tasty or nutritious. They **domesticated** the crop by continually replanting the plants with the most favorable traits such as larger, tastier, and more nutritious cobs. Over many generations of this process, the plant was developed into varieties of the plants we now call maize or corn.

When planted together, corn, beans, and squash complement each other. The cornstalk grows tall and straight, which gives an upright pole for the beanstalk to grow on. Corn uses nutrients like nitrogen to grow, while beans produce nitrogen and put it back into the soil. Both plants help each other. Squash (or pumpkin) vines fill the areas around the stalks of corn. As the squash grows, a low vine creeps along the ground and grows big, broad leaves. These leaves shade the soil, keeping it cool and moist. By blocking the sunlight from hitting the ground, they also stop the light that weeds need to grow. In turn, this reduces the work people do to keep the gardens weed-free.

Corn was a big part of the yearly diet during this era. Corn flour was made by drying freshly picked corn and grinding the dried kernels with a mortar and pestle. Dried corn and corn flour were used to make a multitude of delicious and nutritious dishes, from clay-pot porridges like nausamp to corn cakes infused with the energy and nutrition of berries.

Wampanoag people also knew the proper time to gather valuable food from forests and fields, such as nutrient-rich fiddleheads and ramps (a plant in the onion and garlic family) in the spring and strawberries in the summer. In the fall, they would pick various mushrooms such as Turkey Tail, Chicken of the Woods, or Hen of the Woods. Other parts of the year saw the gathering of nuts from trees, and in the winter, sap was collected from maple and birch trees and boiled to make syrup.

Hunting was another meaningful way to get food and gather resources for clothing and tools. Deer were the most common animals hunted for food. Black bear and smaller animals such as racoons, rabbits, squirrels, and beaver were hunted for meat. Turkeys were hunted year-round.

In summer, people grew or gathered enough food to eat throughout the winter. Fish and meat were smoked to preserve them and fruits and vegetables were dried. People usually had enough corn to eat all winter as well as to plant in the spring.

There was no shortage of food resources in the Wampanoag homelands. Through their ancestral knowledge, they knew how to harvest and sustain all of it.

What did Wampanoag clothing look like in 1620, and how was it made?

Wampanoag clothing came from materials available from the natural resources that surrounded their environment. The most robust and accessible material for clothing was deerskin. Thousands of years ago, Wampanoag and other peoples developed a process for killing a deer and turning its hide into clothing. After killing a deer in a hunt, they skinned the hide from the deer's body and scraped it clean with sharpened bone scrapers made from large animal leg bones. However, if a cleanly scraped hide were simply allowed to set and dry, it would dry into rawhide. Rawhide is useful for many things, but not for clothing.

One process for softening a fresh animal hide is called brain tanning. The hide is scraped, cleaned, and soaked in a mixture of water and the brain of the animal. This releases natural chemicals called tannins that the hide absorbs to make it soft. The clean hide is then stretched on a frame and worked with a paddle-like tool to move the water off the skin. Once completely scraped dry, the hide is smoked. This gives it the tan color and works to keep the hide soft if it gets wet in the rain or while fishing.

Men and women made leather center-seamed moccasins. Leggings made from leather covered the legs on colder days.

Around the waist was tied a breechcloth for men or a skirt for women. On hot days, everyone dressed to stay cool. On cold days, people wore capes of different types of furs. They were worn in a way that left one arm free, which was covered with a "sleeve" made of a smaller fur, such as a lynx or fox. During the winter, they wore clothing made of softened hides with the fur still on and worn inward for warmth. The clothing edges had painted ornamental designs. Seashells became necklaces, bracelets, and other jewelry. Copper was refined and worn as decoration.

Who was Ousamequin?

In 1620, the sachem of the village of Pokanoket, near present-day Bristol, Rhode Island, was Ousamequin, or "Yellow Feather." He is often called Massasoit, which is a title meaning "great leader." Sachems were responsible for taking care of their people, making sure everyone had food, family, and community support.

Sachems led their people by what is called **consensus**. In a consensus, people come to a mutual understanding and general agreement about an issue or a view. They did not "rule" people like kings, but rather their successful leadership depended on good decision-making and the positive influence they held with people. If the community felt their sachem was not being a good leader, they could approach the clan mothers, who would choose another person from the sachem family to be the next sachem.

When the English arrived in Wampanoag country, it was Ousamequin, after consulting with elders, clan mothers, and others, who decided to ally with the English. This allowed the English to stay in Wampanoag country.

What were the first encounters between the English colonists and Wampanoag peoples?

Before the arrival of the *Mayflower* in 1620, English ships were already making yearly visits to this area of North America. Many of the ships traded with Native peoples on the coast. Most of these early encounters seemed friendly, but many times they did not stay that way. Some English captains even tricked some Wampanoag people onto their boats, kidnapping them to become enslaved people back in Europe. Although aware of the dangers the ships could bring, Native peoples continued to trade with the English, taking care to treat them cautiously.

Europeans mainly sought beaver furs for making waterproof beaver felt hats, which Native peoples could supply in good numbers. Wampanoag people knew metal and worked with copper. Copper was used to make many different things, including arrow points, fish hooks, jewelry, beads, mat-sewing needles, and spoons.

The English brought different metals like steel, iron, and brass, which are hard and make good cutting blades and tools. The main trade items Wampanoag people wanted from the English were steel knives and other tools, wool blankets and cloth, and glass bottles and beads.

When the English colonists established their settlement at Plimoth in late 1620, they wrote about seeing and hearing the Wampanoag on more than one occasion. The English feared contact with the Wampanoag. They knew they were not welcome there. As a result, it was a regular practice for English colonists to prepare for conflict with guns and weapons at the sight of a group of Wampanoag people.

The Wampanoag watched through the winter but did not approach until March 1621. According to William Bradford's account, a single Wampanoag man presented himself to the English colonists at Plimoth. He greeted them with the English word "Welcome." He was a Wawenock sachem named Samoset who often visited the Wampanoag people. He had learned to speak some English from early encounters with European traders. Samoset stayed with them from early afternoon until evening, talking to the English and telling them about the plague that had wiped out Patuxet two years earlier, along with many other villages. He arranged for a meeting between the English and Ousamequin, with some of the other Wampanoag leaders who had been watching the town.

Within days, a party of sixty or more Wampanoag men approached the village. They were unwilling to enter Plimoth, but the encounter led to a tentative agreement with the English colonists not to harm each other. This agreement was a mutually beneficial **alliance** between the Wampanoag and English colonists. The English were small in number and in need of help to survive. The Wampanoag saw the English and their weapons as a powerful ally to maintain their territory after the epidemics. After the alliance was established, Wampanoag and the English colonists did not arm themselves for battle when they saw one another.

How did the English colonists and Wampanoag people communicate?

Just six years before the *Mayflower* arrived, English captain Thomas Hunt anchored near the village of Patuxet. He persuaded twenty of the Patuxet Wampanoag to board his ship to trade,

including a young man named Tisquantum. Captain Hunt double-crossed the Wampanoag; kidnapped them, along with seven Nauset people; and took them to Spain to sell as enslaved people.

Tisquantum's sale was blocked by English missionaries, who eventually took him to London, where he learned to speak English. In 1619, Thomas Dermer, another English sea captain, brought Tisquantum home to his village, Patuxet. He found his village devastated by the Great Dying. Everyone had perished.

Tisquantum's ability to speak English was a valuable skill. Traveling with Dermer, Tisquantum went to the island of Noepe, now known as Martha's Vineyard. He then went to the village of Aquinnah. The sachem, Epenow, and his men fought with Dermer and his crew. Most of the crew were killed and Dermer was mortally wounded. Epenow took Tisquantum captive and later sent him to Ousamequin. During his five years of captivity in England, Tisquantum had learned to speak English quite well. As a result, he served as the main translator between Ousamequin and the English colonists.

How did the alliances between the English colonists at Plimoth and the Pokanoket Wampanoags get made?

On March 22, 1621, Samoset and Tisquantum entered Plimoth Plantation asking to meet with colony leaders. Ousamequin was nearby with his brother, Quadequina, and sixty men. They were hoping to enter into an alliance and establish trade. The governor of the colony at the time was John Carver, and he was unwilling to go with Samoset and Tisquantum to meet their leaders outside of the village.

To ensure a good outcome to the meeting, the two sides decided to exchange voluntary hostages. Colonist Edward Winslow volunteered to be held by the Wampanoag men, and he left with Samoset and Tisquantum. In return, the colonists held some of the Wampanoag men. They did this so neither side would harm the other while they talked.

They took Ousamequin to a house to meet with Carver and sat on a green rug piled with cushions. A drummer and trumpeter announced Governor Carver's arrival. He kissed Ousamequin's hand, and Ousamequin returned the gesture, following the formal process that was standard for such occasions.

Neither spoke the other's language, but with Tisquantum's help, they were able to communicate. Ousamequin agreed to the terms of an alliance with the colonists, which included coming to each other's aid against any adversaries in the event they should need it. This alliance was between the English colonists at Plimoth, Ousamequin and his village of Pokanoket, and possibly the other villages Ousamequin was allied with.

The original document recording the alliance no longer exists, but a record was made by William Bradford and Edward Winslow and published in *Mourt's Relation* in 1622. Ousamequin stayed true to the agreement until his death forty years later.

Why did Ousamequin and the colonists agree to an alliance?

The alliance was mutually beneficial to both parties. When the *Mayflower* arrived and the colonists started building a settlement, the Wampanoag leaders debated over what to do. There were over one hundred years of trade encounters ending badly, including the kidnapping and enslaving of Wampanoag people. European diseases took a great toll on their population. This made the Wampanoag fearful, cautious, and watchful upon their arrival. Nevertheless, Ousamequin saw a number of advantages should he form an alliance with the English. The Great Dying of 1616–1619 had wiped out more than three-quarters of the coastal Wampanoag populations in just three years. The disease started far north of Wampanoag country and spread its way down the coast. It turned inland at Patuxet, and stopped at Narragansett Bay, the Narragansett people.

After the devastation of the Great Dying, Narragansett sachems were pressuring Ousamequin to pay them tribute in wampum in exchange for their protection and assistance. Ousamequin resisted, but could not call on as many warriors as before the plague. When the English arrived, he realized that their weapons would give Wampanoag people an advantage should the situation with the Narragansetts get worse.

The English colonists were aware of the situation Ousamequin faced. Plimoth governor William Bradford and fellow colonist Edward Winslow wrote that, "He hath a potent adversary, the Narrowhigansets [Narragansetts] that are at war with him; against whom, he thinks, we may be some strength to him, for our pieces [guns] are terrible unto them."

The English colonists of Plimoth needed assistance to make their settlement successful. Many of them perished during the previous winter. They did not intend for their new settlement to fail. They knew that good relations with the Wampanoag was a large step toward survival.

How did life change for the English colonists in Plimoth after they established contact with the Wampanoag?

After Samoset entered Plimoth, everything changed for the English colonists. They no longer feared being attacked by the Wampanoag. They communicated and developed trade with each other.

Many of the Saints on the *Mayflower* had spent most of their lives in cities. Some of them knew

more about buying food than about producing it. In Plimoth, however, everyone needed to produce all their food. Even with the corn they had stolen and the birds they were able to hunt, the colonists had barely enough supplies for the winter. Before they met any Wampanoag people, many of the colonists perished due to hunger, exposure, and illness.

The colonists brought seeds from the plants that grew in England. However, they were concerned their seeds would not grow. After the alliance, they were able to trade for local indigenous seeds: corn, beans, squash, and pumpkins. Tisquantum came to their village and taught them complementary farming methods like planting corn in mounds, with the beans and squash around them, and using river herring as fertilizer. They also learned what other plants and animals in the region could provide food. This local knowledge was essential to the success of their plantation.

What happened at the feast in Plimoth in 1621?

After a successful first harvest, the English colonists at Plimoth Plantation decided to celebrate with a feast. As part of the celebration, the English colonists took part in recreation, eating, socializing, and firing their weapons. As the day went on,

Ousamequin entered Plimoth with a group of ninety warriors. Following the terms of the alliance, the Wampanoag men laid down their weapons before entering the plantation.

Once inside the village, Ousamequin realized there would not be enough food for everyone, as the Wampanoag had added ninety people to the celebration. He sent four men to kill five deer, which they gave to Governor Bradford and his people. This was a very meaningful gift. Sharing whatever one has, contributing for the overall good of the community, and making sure everyone has enough to eat are strong traditional values that the Wampanoag people followed to ensure everyone's well-being.

Not much is written about the feast itself. We do know the English hosted Ousamequin and his men for three days. There is no historical mention of turkey at this feast, although it could have been there. The English colonists and Ousamequin's men feasted on foods of the time, which included duck, deer, corn, beans, squash, dried berries, and seafood.

What was a "thanksgiving" for English colonists in 1621?

The English colonists celebrated days of thanksgiving as part of their religion. They brought this tradition with them from England. The English colonists viewed their relationship with God as a sacred agreement. A day of thanksgiving was a way of honoring that sacred agreement. An English day of thanksgiving involved fasting, or not eating. They would often spend the entire day silently in prayer.

An English day of thanksgiving is not unlike a religious

holiday, but there are no set dates. They were declared as needed. In England, they were sometimes called in celebration of a victory in war. Whatever the reason, the declaration of a day of thanksgiving meant a celebration, but not the same type of celebration many Americans celebrate today.

Celebrating a harvest with a feast was not uncommon for the English or the Wampanoag, but the feast would not have been thought of as a "thanksgiving" to the English colonists at that time.

What was a "thanksgiving" for Wampanoag and other Native peoples in the region in 1621?

The word "thanksgiving" evolved out of an old English expression that meant "to bestow or grant a grateful thought." Expressions of thanksgiving exist in all cultures. For the Wampanoag people, thanksgivings are feasts or ceremonies and occur annually.

Events such as the arrival of spring (the new year), the ripening of strawberries, and the harvest of corn were cause for celebration and feasting for

the Wampanoag, complete with dancing and ceremonies. The Wampanoag people and other tribes in the area celebrated these expressions of thanksgiving throughout the year. Offering thanks through ceremony, prayer, or sharing food acknowledges the gifts of the natural world that give people life. It is also a reminder of the responsibility of humans to give back to the natural world for what was taken.

All Wampanoag life centers around using resources in a way that leaves plenty for the following years. A common tradition when foraging in the woods for food or medicine is to leave the first plants or trees alone for others to find, or to save them for next year. In return, Wampanoag people express thanks for the things they take from the woods, whether plant or animal life. Some of these thanksgivings are small observations of prayer or song offered by a single person. Others are large ceremonial feasts, such as the Green Corn Festival, celebrated by whole villages in late summer or early fall in honor of the harvest of their largest and most valued crop.

How did life change for the Wampanoag and other Native peoples after the *Mayflower* arrived?

Ousamequin's alliance with the English colonists divided the leadership of the Wampanoag sachems. Not all sachems wanted the English to stay. Some saw Europeans only as bringers of new diseases. Others knew the English only through encounters with slave traders. There were a number of sachems of other villages who did not like the idea of forming an alliance with the English. However, they understood Ousamequin's motivation and agreed to accept his decision. The English broke the terms of the alliance many times over the years, but Ousamequin continued to honor his agreement with them. He thought it was still the best way to handle the relationship with these new people in Wampanoag territory.

Settling Plimoth Plantation in 1620 saw the establishment of Plymouth Colony, which had a governing body back in England. In 1630, Massachusetts Bay Colony was formed in and around

what is now Boston, bringing many ships and thousands of new English colonists.

In the 1630s, English colonists began settling along the Connecticut River. However, the English were competing with Dutch colonists for rights to trade on the river and for a steady supply of beaver furs. Beaver pelts were so valuable to Europeans they were willing to fight to gain control of the trade. This led to the first war of aggression by Europeans against Native peoples in America, known as the Pequot War (1636–37), where the English declared war on the Pequot people to obtain control of the Connecticut River. The war was brutal and weakened the strength of their people to such a degree that they were no longer an obstacle to English expansion in their territory. The Narragansetts allied with the English at

DID YOU KNOW?

The term "New England" is credited first to English whaling captain John Smith, who mapped the region and published a map and book titled *A Description of New England* in 1616. His map identified the harbor and site of the *Mayflower* landing as New Plimoth.

first, but were shocked at the brutality with which the English fought. After the war, the English expanded the Connecticut Colony and started new settlements in the region.

There were so many efforts to claim Indigenous lands and establish colonies that by 1643 the colonists decided to form the United Colonies of New England. This included Massachusetts Bay Colony, Connecticut Colony, New Haven Colony, and Plymouth Colony.

In the years after Ousamequin's death in 1661, the English would continue to settle in Wampanoag territory in greater numbers. Only fifty-five years after the *Mayflower* arrived in North America, the Wampanoag people were seeing much of their land being taken over by the English, and their lives being controlled by colonization.

By this time, Pometacom, Ousamequin's younger son, had become the sachem of Pokanoket. He brought together warriors from all the tribes in southern New England to fight the English settlers to save their homelands and ancient ways of life. Pometacom aimed to drive the English from Wampanoag homelands for good. This war is known as King Philip's War. King Philip is what the English called Pometacom. It is also called the Great Narragansett War or Pometacom's Rebellion, depending on the account. The war ended with the death of Pometacom in 1676.

The effects of disease and war took their toll not just on the Wampanoag people, but on all Native peoples. After King Philip's War, resistance to English colonization in the region diminished greatly. By 1700, nearly all of the region was under the control of the United Colonies of New England and open to English settlement. As the years wore on, English colonies were established all along the east coast and Native territory became smaller. Native communities persisted, but they were now under the constant pressure of colonization, which forced unwanted changes. They had to give up land and traditional spiritual ways; they were enslaved and indentured with the intention of forcing them to become like the English settlers.

Why is the Plimoth feast of 1621 called "the First Thanksgiving"?

The use of the term "the First Thanksgiving" is a mistake of history. The Plimoth feast of 1621 was not called "the First Thanksgiving" or even a "thanksgiving" until more than two hundred years after it happened. English colonists barely left any record of it, and the event was almost unknown until the 1800s. The first person to use the phrase "the First Thanksgiving" was a Boston writer named Alexander Young. In 1841, he published a book containing a letter Edward Winslow had sent to England from Plimoth Plantation in December 1621. Winslow's letter included a short description of the feast of 1621, and Young added a footnote to his book in which he called the event "the First Thanksgiving."

Young made an incorrect assumption about the Plimoth feast based on knowledge of thanksgiving traditions from his own time in the 1800s. At that time,

some Americans now celebrated harvest feasts and called them thanksgivings. These events were family-centered gatherings held around the time of harvest with no specific date.

By the 1820s, magazines had also become popular in America. One magazine, *Godey's Lady's Book*, was run by an editor named Sarah Josepha Hale. Under Hale's leadership, it became one of the most widely circulated magazines in the nation. *Godey's Lady's Book* was so popular that it influenced a lot of American popular

culture. Sarah Josepha Hale wrote articles every November describing thanksgiving feasts. Her descriptions closely resemble the common Thanksgiving meal many Americans eat today. By the time Alexander Young published his book in 1841, thanksgiving feasts were popular and common celebrations in America. Young, however, incorrectly connected the new American tradition popularized by Hale with the feast of 1621 by calling it the "first Thanksgiving" in his footnote.

Young's footnote was copied over and over until it was encountered by Hale. From 1865 onward, Hale and her magazine encouraged Americans to see their thanksgiving feasts as honoring the events of 1621, even though they were not connected. She saw the events at Plimoth as a uniting tale that would bring the country together. The story was very popular, and with Young's mistaken footnote as evidence, no one questioned it. By 1870, schoolbooks were telling the story of the First Thanksgiving, and by the late 1880s, fiction writers were telling a version of the story that became the famous tale we know today. It has been known as "the First Thanksgiving" by Americans ever since.

How and when did Thanksgiving become a national holiday?

Early European thanksgiving events occurred in different areas of the country and resembled the English tradition of a day of prayer and fasting. Spanish explorers in Mexico celebrated a day of thanksgiving in the 1500s. English settlers in the Virginia Colony declared days of thanksgiving before the *Mayflower* arrived in Plimoth. Days of thanksgiving were proclaimed by governors of early English colonies. President George Washington even called a national day of thanksgiving in 1789.

Sarah Josepha Hale was a persuasive writer and her influence grew every year as her magazine grew. Starting in 1849, she wrote to presidents, congress people, and governors about the need for a national Thanksgiving Day. However, for fourteen years none of them listened. The leaders of the time felt it was up to the states to decide for themselves if they wanted to have a Thanksgiving Day or not. As time went on, she continued to press the idea and Thanksgiving Day celebrations held by individual US states grew. By 1854, more than thirty states and US territories were having Thanksgiving celebrations. The celebrations continued even after the outbreak of war between the states in 1861.

In 1863, Hale wrote to William Seward, who was secretary of state for President Abraham Lincoln. Seward and President Lincoln saw declaring a national Thanksgiving Day as a way to try to "heal the wounds of the nation" as a result of the Civil War. On October 3, 1863, President Lincoln made the first of what would become yearly presidential proclamations of a national Thanksgiving Day on the fourth Thursday of each November. Since then, with a few exceptions, it has been a national holiday.

From 1863–1938, Thanksgiving Day was celebrated on the last Thursday of November every year except two. In 1939, President Franklin Roosevelt changed the date to one week earlier to lengthen the Christmas shopping season, which traditionally began the day after Thanksgiving Day. Finally, in 1941, the United States government created a law declaring the fourth Thursday of November as Thanksgiving Day, which is the holiday we all know today.

Why do people in the United States celebrate Thanksgiving today?

Thanksgiving Day remains a favorite holiday in the United States. Americans of all backgrounds observe the holiday in their own ways. It is a paid day off from work for many people and ample reason to get together. It marks the changing of seasons and the beginning of winter. It still serves as a celebration of

harvest. In modern times, Thanksgiving Day is also associated with traditional matchups of college and NFL football teams, along with large televised parades.

The most popular part of Thanksgiving Day is the Thanksgiving meal. Americans cook foods of all types, but Sarah Josepha Hale's description of a thanksgiving meal is still the most common set of dishes served by Americans. As times change, though, menus change. Turkey is still the food most associated with Thanksgiving; for many Americans, Thanksgiving Day is incomplete without it.

Families use the holiday as a yearly gathering of loved ones. Some Americans still associate the Thanksgiving Day holiday with the Plimoth feast of 1621. But there is no "correct" way to celebrate. Over the years, different people have created their own Thanksgiving Day traditions and enjoy the holiday as they choose.

Do other countries have a Thanksgiving holiday?

Countries and cultures around the world have their own thanksgiving celebrations, and for each of them it can mean something different. Today there are versions of Thanksgiving Day celebrated in many countries around the world. Canada's harvest celebration dates to 1578. China's Mid-Autumn Festival celebrates the harvest and dates back to 3,000 years ago. In Japan, they celebrate the season's first rice harvest with a ritual offering of thanks during a holiday called Kinrō Kansha no Hi, or Labor Thanksgiving Day, which goes back more than 2,000 years. Every September, South Koreans celebrate a day of thanksgiving for harvest and ancestors on a holiday called Chuseok. In Germany, the first Sunday of October includes celebrations, parades, fireworks, music, and dancing dedicated to a harvest celebration known as Erntedankfest.

Do Native peoples celebrate Thanksgiving?

Native peoples see the American Thanksgiving Day holiday differently than other citizens, depending on their tribe or nation. Native peoples today represent 574 recognized nations. Each tribe or nation has its own culture and language based on its homelands. Therefore, every tribe and nation is different and has its own beliefs and history. Many Wampanoag and other Native peoples met by colonists in the 1600s do not celebrate the day. For them, associating Thanksgiving Day with the arrival of the *Mayflower* as Americans often do reminds them of the disease, slavery, and war their ancestors endured. From their perspective, the country was not "born." Instead, their ancestors' homelands were invaded. Many of these tribes have a day of prayer or mourning rather than a feast around that time of year.

Native peoples in other parts of the country do not have the same history associated with Wampanoag people or other east coast tribes. They are aware that the current holiday has nothing to do with the landing of the *Mayflower* or the feast of 1621 at

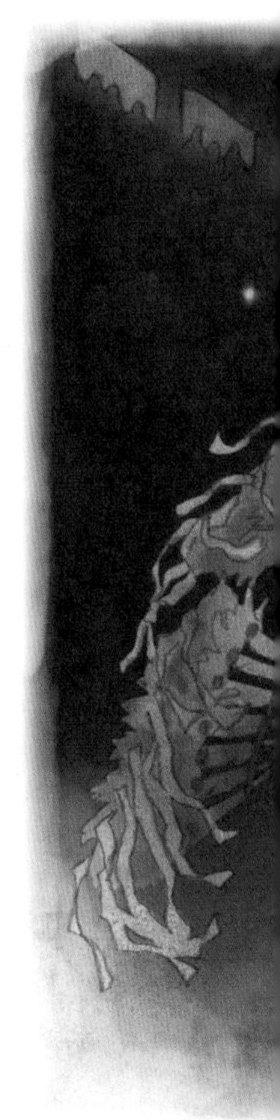

Plimoth. They have no problem celebrating the national holiday in much the same way as the rest of the United States does, with celebration, food, and football. Other tribes view the holiday as strictly an American holiday and they do not celebrate it, and others have incorporated the holiday into their ceremonial calendar.

What are holidays that honor Native history?

The United States has no official holiday that honors Native history. In 1915, the Congress of the American Indian Association ordered its director, Reverend Sherman Coolidge of the Arapaho people, to declare the second Saturday of each May as American Indian Day. They also appealed to make Native peoples citizens of the United States. To get the day approved, Red Fox James of the Blackfoot people rode horseback from state to state, getting sign-offs from state governments. He succeeded in getting twenty-four states to sign, but the US government never created the holiday. Still, individual states honor Native peoples with state holidays such as American Indian Day, which began in New York in 1916.

In the late 1970s, Congress created different laws, and presidents made declarations, of various days, weeks, or months in honor of the heritage of Native peoples in America. Nothing was permanent, however. In 1990, President George H.W. Bush approved a resolution calling the month of November National American Indian Heritage Month. In 2009, President Barack Obama signed legislation designating the Friday immediately after Thanksgiving Day each year as Native American Heritage Day; the same year, he designated November as National Native American Heritage Month in honor of the history and continued existence of America's Native peoples.

Another change is a popular unofficial holiday called Indigenous Peoples' Day. Indigenous Peoples' Day is a response to the Columbus Day federal holiday signed into law in 1968 that falls on the second Monday of October. Many Native peoples do not recognize Columbus Day for a multitude of reasons. The biggest reason is that it does not honor Native history, but rather European colonists. Without an official Native holiday, many Native nations, local, and state governments began celebrating holidays in honor of Native peoples on the same date as Columbus Day. The first US state to change Columbus Day was South Dakota in 1990 with a holiday called Native American Day. In 1992, the city of Berkeley, California, became the first city to officially replace Columbus Day with Indigenous Peoples' Day on their calendar. There are currently eight states and over 130 cities in the US that have officially adopted Indigenous Peoples' Day to replace Columbus Day. Other states like California and Nevada celebrate Native American Day and Tennessee celebrates American Indian Day, all in the month of September.

In recent years an increasing wave of organizations, schools, towns, cities, and states have officially replaced Columbus Day on their calendars with Indigenous Peoples' Day in honor of the Native peoples of the United States. Indigenous Peoples' Day involves educational events. Many Native peoples share their culture by speaking, singing, dancing, and other expressions of art and history. The emerging holiday is a great way to educate honestly about the history and continued existence of tribes and nations that live here today.

INDIGENOUS PEOPLES DAY

INDIGENOUS PEOPLES'
DAY

Glossary

Alliance: a formal agreement between two groups for a common purpose
Brackish water: a mix of salt and fresh water
Colonist: a member of a colony
Colonization: the processes to gain control of land and resources to transfer a population to a foreign territory whether occupied or not
Colony: a group of people who leave their home country to form a settlement in a different land
Complementary farming: the practice of planting different crops together to increase production
Consensus: general agreement of opinion or plan going forward
Currency: something of value being used in trade or exchange; money
Discover: to see, learn of, or find out, usually for the first time
Domesticate: to adapt a plant to be beneficial to human beings
Estuary: a part of the river that meets the sea's tide
Flint knapping: the shaping of certain types of stone to create tools
Foundational: relating to the basis or groundwork
Hybridize: to combine two unlike products to create something new
***Mayflower* Compact:** the first agreement of self-governance between the men on the *Mayflower*
Pilgrim: a person making a long journey, often for religious reasons